MILLBURY PUBLIC LIBRARY

D1105389

A BEACON BIOGRAPHY

Carly Rae

JEPSEN

Heidi Krumenauer

PURPLE TOAD
PUBLISHING

P.O. Box 631
Kennett Square, Pennsylvania 19348
www.purpletoadpublishing.com

J
B JEPSEN 9/14

Copyright © 2014 by Purple Toad Publishing, Inc. All rights reserved. No part of this book may be reproduced without written permission from the publisher. Printed and bound in the United States of America.

Printing   1   2   3   4   5   6   7   8   9

A Beacon Biography

Big Time Rush
Carly Rae Jepsen
Drake
Harry Styles of One Direction
Jennifer Lawrence
Kevin Durant
Robert Griffin III (RG3)

Publisher's Cataloging-in-Publication Data
Krumenauer, Heidi
  Carly Rae Jepsen / Heidi Krumenauer
    p. cm. – (A beacon biography)
Includes bibliographic references and index.
ISBN: 978-1-62469-024-2 (library bound)
1. Jepsen, Carly Rae, 1985–. 2. Singers—Canada—Biography—Juvenile literature.   I. Title.
  ML3930.J47 2013
  782.42164092—dc23
                                                                                        2013934695

eBook ISBN: 9781624690259

ABOUT THE AUTHOR: Heidi Krumenauer has written more than 1,200 newspaper and magazine articles. Her first book, *Why Does Grandma Have a Wibble?*, was published in 2007. She is also the author of several celebrity biographies, including *Lady Gaga* and *Harry Styles of One Direction*. Krumenauer graduated from the University of Wisconsin-Platteville in 1991 with a degree in Technical Communications Management. She holds a position in upper management with a Fortune 400 insurance company. She and her husband, Jeff, raise their two sons, Noah and Payton, in Southern Wisconsin.

PUBLISHER'S NOTE: The data in this book has been researched in depth, and to the best of our knowledge is factual. Although every measure is taken to give an accurate account, Purple Toad Publishing makes no warranty of the accuracy of the information and is not liable for damages caused by inaccuracies. This story has not been authorized or endorsed by Carly Rae Jepsen.

Printed by Lake Book Manufacturing, Chicago, IL

CONTENTS

Carly Rae Jepsen

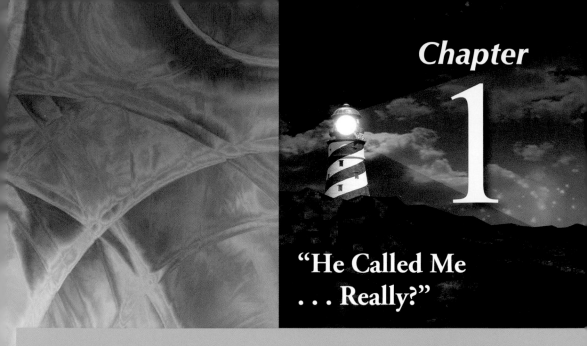

It's very likely that Carly Rae Jepsen will never forget the frantic phone call from her younger sister, Katie, who told her that Justin Bieber was using Twitter to promote her song. "She said, 'Justin has just tweeted about your song.' And I was like, 'Justin?' She's like, 'Justin Bieber.' I was like, 'What?' Then I went and checked it out and, in fact, she was right, and then my whole world changed," Jepsen told *RyanSeacrest.com.*

According to *Rolling Stone Magazine,* Justin Bieber, a fellow Canadian, was home for the holidays (doing dishes in his mother's kitchen) in Stratford, Ontario, in December 2011 when he heard "Call Me Maybe" on the radio. He immediately liked what he heard and tweeted: "Call me maybe by Carly Rae Jepsen is possibly the catchiest song I've ever heard lol." "Call Me Maybe" began to climb the iTunes Singles chart after Bieber's tweet went out to his 17.5 million Twitter followers.

"I was listening to the radio and her song came on, and I was like, 'Who is this?'" Bieber told Ellen DeGeneres in March 2012 during a joint appearance with Jepsen. "I feel as an artist I have a responsibility to pay it forward. When I was home in Canada, I

Bieber and Jepsen appeared on **The Ellen DeGeneres Show** *in March 2012.*

heard Carly and I became a fan and felt like I could help her the way Usher once helped me. The good news is she is a superstar."

Jepsen was on tour with the group Hanson when she learned that Bieber wanted to sign her to Schoolboy Records, the company he runs with music executive Scooter Braun. But instead of spreading the news to everyone, Jepsen held her secret close. "I hinted to my parents, but I didn't tell my brother and sister," she said. "I kept it all to myself, just in case it didn't happen. I didn't want to be the girl who cried wolf and was like, 'Hey, I'm signing with Justin Bieber,' and then never mind."

Thankfully for Jepsen, the deal went through. In February 2012, Schoolboy Records announced that Carly Rae Jepsen was the newest artist to sign with the label. "Every once in a while you stumble upon an artist that really fills a gap in the industry. Carly is that artist," Braun said. "Not only is she kind, sweet and hardworking but she is truly a genuine talent. She had me sold from the moment she told me she sees herself as a sexy hippie."

Not many people have "The Biebs" in their corner. Jepsen considers herself lucky. "I had never branched outside of Canada and had no idea how to do that and then one miraculous day, Justin called," she told DeGeneres. "It's just nice in general that he has been such a big supporter. He changed the game for me and I don't know what I would be doing had he not come along and put his influence behind 'Call Me Maybe.' It really changed my world, so I'm very grateful that we're a team. My sister is adamant that one way or another we're going to have a hang session with Justin though. I'm like: 'Ooookay, I'll see what I can do.' "

Jepsen and Bieber have remained friends.

The welcome sign in Mission, British Columbia, greets visitors as they cross the border.

Communities in Bloom

Welcome to Mission

PROUD SISTER CITY TO OYAMA JAPAN

Carly Rae Jepsen was born in Mission, British Columbia, Canada, on November 11, 1985. Her parents are Alexandra and Larry Jepsen. She has a brother, Colin Jepsen, and a sister, Katie Jepsen. Although her parents divorced when she was young, she told *Sunday World*, "[they] remarried, but they were both really smart with their decisions of who they married and I got really good stepparents." Her stepmother is Patty Jepsen, and her stepfather is Ron Lanzarotta.

"Since I was seven, music has been a big part of my life," Carly Rae said. "At every party or family event, I would always find my way to the stage."

Her parents also recognized her musical talent at a young age. "I can still remember when she was about three and her mom and I would be strumming a guitar with her and she'd be on pitch," Larry Jepsen said. He sang James Taylor songs to her before bed. Her mother taught her the lyrics to Leonard Cohen songs. Ella Fitzgerald and Van Morrison were other childhood musical influences. "Music was the way I connected with

Snapshots of young Carly Rae

everyone and my family encouraged that in me," Jepsen says in her web site biography. "I grew up listening to what my parents listened to, which were more folk-inspired artists. Then I moved to the city, started going out with friends and listening to different music that made me realize I had a strong attraction to pop—artists like Robyn and Dragonette," she said.

Jepsen recalls writing her first song when she was nine years old. "I wrote a protest song called 'Cutting Down the Big Tree.' It was so bad. It was like, 'We're cutting down the big tree.' I think that was the main hook."

Singing wasn't the only thing Jepsen enjoyed. She also loved being in front of the camera or on stage. She was never shy when the family would make videos to send to her grandparents in Winnipeg, Manitoba. In high school, it didn't surprise anyone that she had roles in *Annie*, *The Wiz*, and *Grease*. "I remember when I was in a play about little orphan Annie in high school. At the end of the weeklong production I was in tears. I said to my parents: 'Oh my gosh, what if that's it? I really want to do this. What if that was my big moment in life?' It made me realize that fast fame would be too much pressure and that it would be great if I could have a natural, slow rise."

After graduating from Heritage Park Secondary School in Mission, Jepsen began performing at local pubs. While she was attending the Canadian College of Performing Arts in Victoria, she had dreams of being a Broadway star. That quickly changed when she received her first guitar for Christmas at the age of seventeen. She started writing songs the first week she had it. She considered

Jepsen in her teen years

becoming a music teacher, but her real love of singing her own music won out.

Jepsen's parents stood behind her decision from the beginning. "I think realistically as parents we were pretty proud of her to try something as high risk as this for her career. Go for it and do it while you're young so you don't have any regrets," Larry told CBC Radio in August 2012.

Jepsen poses for promo shots for **Canadian Idol.**

Chapter

3

Call Her Famous

By 2007, Jepsen was tired of playing in pubs; she wanted more for her simple life. Still, when auditions for *Canadian Idol* were held in her town, she wasn't very excited about the opportunity. "The day of the audition, I remember thinking, 'I could have a long bath, or I could just go audition.'" Thankfully, she took the chance because she ended up as a contestant on the fifth season of the reality television show. "Actually, it was sort of a last-minute push by my high school drama teacher to go and audition for that show," she confessed. For weeks, she rehearsed her songs and prepared to sing them in front of a panel of four judges.

"When I saw the reality show of *Idol*, I was like, 'That's not how it's going to happen, that can't be it for me,'" she admitted. "But it really was a game-changer, and I have no regrets in doing that show. I think from that experience I learned that it is important to not knock down different opportunities, because it might just be the thing that really helps you, or gives you that leg up that you need."

After weeks of competition, Jepsen made it to the top three finalists. "It gave me my first fifteen minutes of fame," she told

Jepsen played her guitar and sang during her audition for Canadian Idol.

CollegeGloss.com. "I think what was nice about not winning was that I was able to put out songs that were original rather than covers. It gave me the hunger to show my individuality and show that I wanted to write songs!"

Shortly after *Idol,* Jepsen landed a record deal with MapleMusic/Fontana North in Ontario. Later she signed with 604 Records in British Columbia. In 2008, her folk-based album, *Tug of War,* debuted. The title track earned her a Canadian Radio Music Award.

Jepsen received many other accolades in Canada, including Juno Award nominations in 2010 for Songwriter of the Year and Best New Artist, and a 2010 MuchMusic Video Award nomination for UR Fave New Artist.

In February 2012, she released her EP (extended play), *Curiosity,* in Canada. The compilation included "Call Me Maybe," which had already climbed to the top of the Billboard Canadian Hot 100 chart. After Bieber's tweet, it gained international fame. Jepsen says it was surreal to know her song hit #1 on the U.S. Billboard Hot 100. "I still honestly can't believe we had nine weeks [on the U.S. charts]," she said. Jepsen wrote the song with two friends, Tavish Crowe and Josh Ramsay. "It was written for the pure joy of writing rather than making a hit. I think we all felt like it came together easy, which is always a good sign. But that's about it. I didn't know it was going to be the song that changed my life."

Again, thanks to the interest of Bieber, a "Call Me Maybe" video went viral. In the video, Bieber, Selena Gomez, Ashley Tisdale, Big Time Rush, and other pop stars lip-synced the song. It had more than a million views in its first twenty-four hours.

A fan posted the video to Jepsen's web site, but she didn't believe it was Bieber. "I first saw Justin and Selena's video along with everyone else when it was posted on Carlos Pena's YouTube channel," she said. "I thought, 'Wow, that boy looks a lot like Justin Bieber.' Had no idea. And then I watched it three more times because it had Selena Gomez stuff ahead of it, and I was like, 'I think that might be him!' It was a pretty crazy moment, for sure."

Two days later, Jepsen met Bieber at a recording studio in Los Angeles. "We spent some time talking and hearing songs from his new album, and on the fourth song he's like, 'Do you like this song? If you like it, I was thinking maybe you would wanna sing on it,'" she said. Thirty minutes later, Jepsen was in a recording studio with Bieber and his band, watching from the sound booth. "He'd already recorded his part, so I was harmonizing with his parts," she said. "He was there for parts of it, [but] at one point they left the room because I'm sure they could sense I was nervous."

Jepsen takes time to meet her fans and sign autographs.

Chapter 4

Call Her Busy

On September 18, 2012, with "Call Me Maybe" still at the height of its popularity, her full-length pop album, *Kiss*, was released worldwide. New to this album was a star-studded crew helping her with the vocals. Redfoo of LMFAO and Matthew Koma wrote one of her favorite tracks, "This Kiss." When paparazzi swarmed her at the airport, Redfoo saved her. "We became fast friends, chatted about music and agreed to write a song together. He was touring with Matthew Koma, and the next two weeks the three of us proceeded to write a song over phone calls and e-mails and, ta-da, it was done," Jepsen said.

Her song "Good Time" with Owl City started moving up the charts in the fall of 2012. The track appeared both on Owl City's album *The Midsummer Station* and on Jepsen's *Kiss*. Scooter Braun initially played the track for her, and she instantly liked it, but she didn't know that Adam Young of Owl City wanted her to sing with him. "When Adam reached out, I was in Canada for the Juno [Awards], so I recorded my vocal at 3 A.M. It wasn't till the video shoot that we were actually introduced."

Jepsen is pleased with the reception of *Kiss*. "I definitely wanted to make a pop album," she says in her web site biography. "My love affair with pop music has been growing stronger and stronger each year. I'm a bit of a [hippie] at heart so it's kind of like flower-child pop. My intention was to make an album that really felt like me and shows what I have to offer the music world. It's inspired by Robyn and The Cars and it's all about matters of the heart."

Eleven days after her album was released, Jepsen hit the road to tour with Justin Bieber. "I have been watching all of my favorite live performances. Cyndi Lauper, Madonna, Feist. It makes me pumped to dream up my own live show," she told the *Arizona Republic* in September 2012. Jepsen had a preview of her tour with Bieber earlier in 2012, when they entertained international crowds. "I did two shows with Justin. One in London and one in Mexico

Touring in Mexico City

Jepsen tours in concert with Bieber.

City, and all I can say is, like, 'Wow.' They were huge—300,000 people in Mexico City. I was speechless."

Jepsen definitely has a huge fan base, and, she says, "I love them right back!" She explained, "In the song 'Call Me Maybe,' the line 'before you came into my life I missed you so bad' was originally about a boy, but now when I sing that song I sing it for the audience because I mean it. Having all of the supporters that I do, it seems too lucky to be fair!"

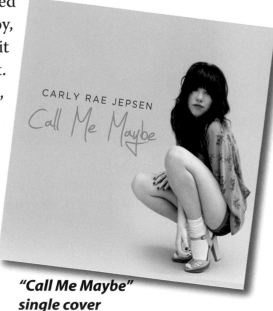

"Call Me Maybe" single cover

As an overnight sensation, Jepsen had little time to adjust to her wild popularity. In June 2012, her grueling schedule put an impossible strain on her relationship with the boy who had inspired "Call Me Maybe." She and Jordi Ashworth,

Carly Rae Jepsen with her band. Left to right: Jared Manierka (keys), Tavish Crowe (guitar), Solomon Standing (bass), and Nik Pesut (drums).

an architect student, had been dating for a year when she called it off.

She said it was hard to believe that just two years earlier she had been touring Canada in a soccer mom van with the guys who are still in her band. "I was paying them with home-cooked dinners because that's all I could afford, and rushing to my merchandising table to sell shirts afterwards," she told *The [London] Sun.* "These days, my energy gets to go into other aspects, like creatively—what do we want the merchandising to look like and how do we take it on?"

With her new fame, Jepsen is spending more time performing on stage, yet she's still trying to get used to it. "It is always a little nerve-wracking, but it is only nerve-wracking for the first 30 seconds. It is kind of like when you meet someone for the first time . . . there is that initial thrill, and then when you get to know them you can be yourself," she says. She admits that carrying a small knickknack or shaking hands with her band mates helps her feel like she has a little extra luck on stage. And when her fans start singing along, she melts into the moment, calling it "really magical."

Jepsen with Jordi Ashworth

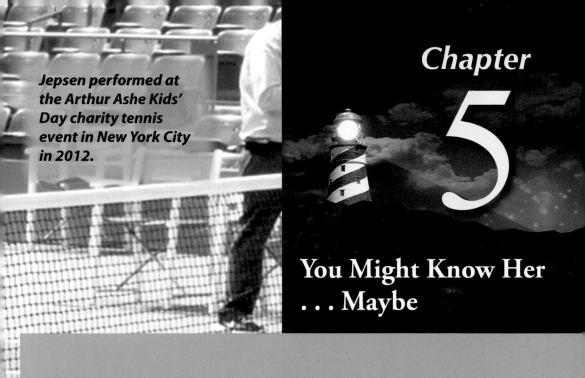

Jepsen performed at the Arthur Ashe Kids' Day charity tennis event in New York City in 2012.

Chapter 5

You Might Know Her . . . Maybe

Jepsen's songs are played on the radio repeatedly throughout the day. People hear her so much, they might feel as if they know her. But do they really? When this superstar singer isn't traveling around the country performing on stage, she enjoys simple things like hiking and spending time in her kitchen. "I really like to cook. One of my favorite things to make is homemade sushi. And I bake cookies and muffins," she says. Her favorite meal, though, is mushroom risotto.

Jepsen is a fan of playing chess. And since she doesn't have a television, she reads a lot of books, which she says helps her with her songwriting. She admits she was obsessed with *The Hunger Games* series. "Other than that I just like to chill with my family and friends," she told *CollegeGloss.com.* Often that time includes house parties with great music and dance competitions.

"Conversely, Carly Rae chose a matching tartan skirt worn with white hightop sneakers to perform at a charity tennis event in New York City. Her playful styling even involved a colorful plastic bracelet."

Jepsen visits home for the holidays and she even makes time to tell Santa Claus what she wants for Christmas.

Living on the road might seem glamorous, but when she's touring, Jepsen misses home. She told Vancouver's *Globe and Mail* in September 2012 that she considered herself homeless when she gave up her Vancouver condominium after not being there for several months. She says she has to look at her hotel key card in the morning to figure out where she is. She looked forward to trading in the hotel rooms for time with her parents in Mission and Maple Ridge, British Columbia, over the holidays. "I'm really looking forward to Christmas, just for the fact that I'll be back in Canada, in my pajamas, not changing for a week, and just chilling with my family."

What about dating, though? The title "Call Me Maybe" gives the impression that Jepsen doesn't have a hard time approaching guys. She says it's quite the opposite. "I have never been brave enough to use pick-up lines or ask guys to hang out . . . it is just so awkward to me!" she said. She told *People* that she likes guys with confidence, but no one over the top or cocky. She also admits that she loves spontaneous dates that include a homemade dinner.

Jepsen enjoys posing for photographs with her fans.

In 2013, Jepsen was chosen to be the new Candie's girl to model their products.

Jepsen says that it's the quiet times, when she's alone, that are the most productive and meaningful to her music. "I find if I go outside I am always inspired," she said. "I think going on a long walk and bringing a notebook is always a great way to get ideas."

Jepsen has enjoyed the beginnings of what appears to be a very long career, but she is already thinking about the next ten years. "Whatever it is, it's meant to be! I don't want to plan it out. As long as I am songwriting I will be a happy woman," she told *CollegeGloss.com.* But what should her fans expect from her over the next few years? Her answer is simple: more music! "I have a feeling I am going to be embracing the pop world in a big way because my love affair with it is increasing! Expect the unexpected!"

Jepsen's new-look red hair is sent flying as she sings onstage in Florida, July, 2013.

1985   Carly Rae Jepsen is born in Mission, British Columbia, Canada, on November 11.

2002   She receives a guitar for her birthday and starts writing music.

2007   She auditions for *Canadian Idol* and is one of the top three finalists.

2008   Her first album, *Tug of War*, is released in Canada.

2010   Jepsen is nominated for numerous awards, including the 2010 Juno Award for Songwriter of the Year and Best New Artist, and a 2010 MuchMusic Video Award for UR Fave New Artist. She wins a Canadian Radio Music Award for the single "Tug of War."

2011   "Call Me Maybe" is released as a single in Canada in September. Justin Bieber hears the song on Canadian radio and tweets about it.

2012   Jepsen's EP, *Curiosity*, is released in Canada in February. Her full-length album *Kiss* is released worldwide in the fall. She tours with Justin Bieber. She receives an American Music Award for New Artist of the Year. She performs on Dick Clark's New Year's Rockin' Eve.

2013   Jepsen launches her Summer Kiss Tour.
Releases her version of *The Little Mermaid* song, *Part Of Your World*.

Albums

2012   *Kiss*
        Curiosity (EP, Canadian release)
2008   *Tug of War* (Canadian release)

Hit Singles

"Call Me Maybe"
"Good Time" (with Owl City)
"This Kiss"
"Part of Your World"

Books

Bieber, Justin. *Just Getting Started.* New York: HarperCollins, 2012.

Louise, Dorothy. *Carly Rae Jepsen—Unabridged Guide.* London: Tebbo, 2012.

Works Consulted

Ballhorn, Kelly. "Carly Rae Jepsen Recalls How She Found Out Justin Bieber Liked Her Song" [AUDIO]. *RyanSeacrest.com,* March 6, 2012.

Brody, Caitlin. "Carly Rae Jepsen, The Singer of 'Call Me Maybe,' Dishes on *The Hunger Games* and What It's Like to Be a Part of Justin Bieber's Crew." *Glamour,* March 9, 2012. http://www.glamour.com/entertainment/blogs/obsessed/2012/03/carly-rae-jepsen-the-singer-of.html

"Carly Rae Jepsen and Justin Bieber on *The Ellen Show:* Bieber Previews 'Boyfriend.' " *The Huffington Post* (VIDEO), March 23, 2012. http://www.huffingtonpost.com/2012/03/23/carly-rae-jepsen-justin-bieber-ellen-show-bieber-previews-boyfriend_n_1375275.html

"Carly Rae Jepsen Signs to Schoolboy Records/Interscope, Run by Scooter Braun and Justin Bieber." *PRNewswire,* February 29, 2012. http://www.prnewswire.com/news-releases/carly-rae-jepsen-signs-to-schoolboy-recordsinterscope-run-by-scooter-braun-and-justin-bieber-140841643.html

Chi, Paul. "Carly Rae Jepsen Calls Her New Man 'Really Great.' " *People,* September 26, 2012. http://www.people.com/people/article/0,,20624426,00.html

Dunn, Gaby. "Carly Rae Jepsen Writes a Song You Can't Escape." *The New York Times,* September 27, 2012. http://www.nytimes.com/2012/09/30/magazine/carly-rae-jepsen-call-me-maybe.html

Getlen, Larry. "How Bieber Made Carly Rae Jepsen a Sensation." *The New York Post,* May 27, 2012. http://www.nypost.com/p/entertainment/music/the_call_before_the_storm_k1S5hCSzAnleC90sFnfSNL

Lederman, Marsha. "Can Carly Rae Jepsen Prove She's More than a One-megahit Wonder?" *The [Vancouver] Globe and Mail,* September 17, 2012. http://www.theglobeandmail.com/arts/music/can-carly-rae-jepsen-prove-shes-more-than-a-one-megahit-wonder/article4550166/

McGuire, Caroline. "Carly Rae Jepsen: I Toured in a Soccer Mom's Van, Now I'm Playing Stadiums." *The [London] Sun,* September 11, 2012. http://www.thesun.co.uk/sol/homepage/showbiz/music/4531840/Call-Me-Maybe-star-Carly-Rae-Jepsen-on-fame-Justin-Bieber-and-new-album-Kiss.html

Masley, Ed. "Carly Rae Jepsen Talks 'Call Me Maybe,' Justin Bieber." *The Arizona Republic,* September, 10, 2012. http://www.azcentral.com/arizonarepublic/arizonaliving/articles/2012/09/05/20120905carly-rae-jepsen-interview-phoenix-justin-bieber.html

"Not Just Maybe: Talking to Carly Rae Jepsen's Parents." Interview with CBC Radio One, *The Early Edition,* August 6, 2012. http://www.cbc.ca/player/Radio/Local+Shows/British+Columbia/ID/2264385285/?sort=MostRecent

Parker, Lyndsey. "Carly Rae Jepsen Talks *Canadian Idol* Beginnings." Yahoo! Music, August 29, 2012. http://music.yahoo.com/blogs/reality-rocks/carly-rae-jepsen-talks-canadian-idol-beginnings-181455846.html

Powell, Hannah Lyons. "Carly Rae Jepsen Splits from 'Call Me Maybe' Boyfriend." *Glamour,* August 28, 2012. http://www.glamourmagazine.co.uk/celebrity/celebrity-news/2012/08/28/carly-rae-jepsen-splits-call-me-maybe-boyfriend

Robinson, Annie. "Call Me Maybe: CGS Interview with Carly Rae Jepsen." *CollegeGloss.com,* March 12, 2012. http://www.collegegloss.com/2012/03/cgs-exclusive-interview-with-music.html

Vena, Jocelyn. "Carly Rae Jepsen Expects Justin Bieber Tour to Be a 'Whoa Moment.'" *MTV News,* July 30, 2012. http://www.mtv.com/news/articles/1690792/carly-rae-jepsen-justin-bieber-tour.jhtml

On the Internet

Carly Rae Jepsen Official Web Site

    www.carlyraemusic.com

Carly Rae Jepsen on Facebook

    www.facebook.com/Carlyraejepsen

GLOSSARY

aghast—Shocked or amazed.

audition—To try out for an acting, singing, or dancing role.

dynamo—A person full of energy and enthusiasm.

heroine—A female hero.

indie—A movie made by an independent company instead of a major studio.

naïve—Innocent.

nomination—To be considered for a position or an award.

red-eye—A flight usually between the hours of midnight and 6 a.m.

tomboy—A girl who is more interested in the traditional fashion, activities, and behavior of boys.

PHOTO CREDITS: All photos—cc-by-sa-2.0. Every measure has been taken to find all copyright holders of material used in this book. In the event any mistakes or omissions have happened within, attempts to correct them will be made in future editions of the book.

MILLBURY PUBLIC LIBRARY

9-14

MILLBURY PUBLIC LIBRARY